Simple Living Manual

C.Z. Lazarus

Published by C.Z. Lazarus, 2021.

While every precaution has been taken in the preparation of this book, the publisher assumes no responsibility for errors or omissions, or for damages resulting from the use of the information contained herein.

SIMPLE LIVING MANUAL

First edition. June 19, 2021.

Copyright © 2021 C.Z. Lazarus.

ISBN: 979-8201019624

Written by C.Z. Lazarus.

Also by C.Z. Lazarus

Spirituality Over Suicidal Depression
The Interactive Book of Magic for Beginners
Energy Ball Bible
Control the Fire Element with Your Mind
You are the Magic Wand
Basic Pendulum Magic for Divination
Dark Energy Mastery Manual
Christos Magick
Enochian Handbook on Dark Wizardry
The Secret Seal of Solomon, Clavicula Magus
Energy Harmony Magic
Starsoul Wizardry Handbook
Reconstructing the Mind for True Spirituality
Arcane Magic for Beginners
The Psychic Witch Handbook
Cast a Magic Circle
A Beginner's Guide to Demonic Possession & Exorcism
Simple Living Manual

Watch for more at https://www.charlzdelacruz.com/.

Table of Contents

For Cristina

Introduction

Simple Living Manual is a life manual that teaches the art of simple living. These days, life has become burdensome with lots of stress, and many people want to declutter their lives to be free. The way of simple living is an art, and it is a beautiful way to live. Instead of being bombarded with so many things, we can choose to only welcome and keep only the things we need and those that are special to us. This approach will create more time and meaning in life.

Simple Living Manual is a beginner's guide to the art of simple living. If you are feeling heavily stressed and trapped, now is the time to free yourself from all the things that tie you down and make you feel miserable. Living simply is not a new approach to life, but it is actually the most natural way humans can live — just as the way our ancestors did. In fact, when Jesus walked on Earth, He also lived a simple and minimalist lifestyle.

This manual teaches the ins and outs of the art of simple living — yes, simple living is an art. Today, many people are turning to ways that can help declutter their lives from all the noise and garbage that ruin the quality of life. Indeed, we now live in a world of material excess and uncontrollable desires. Simple living reminds us of what truly matters in life, and it shows us a way of living that is light, peaceful, calm, relaxing, and full of joy and meaning.

Simple Living Manual gives the foundation that you need to start living and enjoying a simple and minimalist lifestyle. Now is the time to free yourself from the things that bring you down and give you so much stress. In fact, we are not just talking about things, but also negative people. Indeed, simple living is a way of life that can heal and make you feel good again about being alive. To live simply is to live magically with peace of mind and heart.

Are you ready for a life-changing adventure? If yes, then let me now welcome you into the world of simply living — a life of beauty, meaning, peace, and love — the life that you deserve.

What is Simple Living?

Simple living does not need flowery words for it is in and of itself already pure and beautiful. Contrary to the demands of the modern world, simple living calls us back to what we used to be and how we used to live — simple — simple and true.

Simple living means living simply and minimally. These days, the minimalism movement is very popular as people are starting to notice the faults that are inherent in the usual lifestyle of the modern world. It should be clarified that simple living does not mean that you are living a poor life. Simple living calls us to living a life with intention, consciousness, and meaning.

Do not let the terms confuse you. After all, the meaning of any term depends on how you define and understand it. Minimalism is also simple living. It is also worth noting that minimalism started in the genre of art, which is all why simple living is also considered an art — an art of living.

Do you feel so much clutter in your life? Do you feel as if there is so much stress around you that you cannot breathe? If yes, then know that there is a way to solve all these problems. The modern world tells us to keep adding things to be happy. However, the problem with this approach is that it usually ends up making us feel miserable. No wonder obesity is a very common problem these days.

However, obesity is not the only problem. In fact, obesity only shows that the approach of the modern world can be disastrous. It may seem all good and well but once you look closer into it, you will see just how terrible that approach has made your life as a whole.

Simple living allows us to breathe. Moreover, the good news is that simple living does not involve adding, so you do not need to take another hour of work. In fact, simple living is more about removing and non-doing. This means that you can live the art of simple living already right now at this very moment.

If you take this shift in lifestyle and start to live simply and minimally, you will experience the beauty of this lifestyle immediately. From there, you will be in a much better position to decide if it is the kind of lifestyle that you want for yourself or not. Chances are that you will like it and that you are going to fall in love with it. Why? Because simple living will give you the space that you need to breathe and become peaceful. It will bring harmony into your life and allow you to live a truly meaningful life.

Less is More Philosophy

Simple living believes that less is more. You should realize that every new thing that you add into your life would require responsibility on your part — and this would necessarily mean time. Hence, if you notice, those who have so many things to bother with are often the ones who are so busy and have no time — sometimes not even the time to spend with their loved ones. The things that they have end up owning them instead of the other way around. If this is the kind of life you have, then there is a high chance that you are one of the many sad and miserable people in the world.

There are people who do not understand the wisdom behind the less is more approach because they are not seeing it from the right standpoint. Less is more means that you now have more time to do the things that you truly love and spend more time with the people who matter to you. Less is more also means more value for yourself and others , serenity in life, and goodness in your heart. It means more time to relax and have fun and the ability to let go of the things that make you feel miserable. It is about letting go of the things that you do not need and filling your life only with the things that make you happy.

When we fill our life with meaningless things and those that we do not need, soon enough, we may feel suffocated. But, when we free ourselves of these things, we start to breathe and appreciate life more. The less is more approach allows us to appreciate our life and make us experience that we are truly alive and not merely existing in this world.

Having more things gives us less time. Every new thing that we add into our life would demand our attention and time. Imagine having so many of these things, and you will surely end up with so little time to live your life. If we think about it, so many people are stressed out and unhappy with their lives. Being busy has become a new state of mind. It is good if you are busy with good things, but if you are busy dealing with meaningless things and those that you do not enjoy much, then no wonder you would end up sad and miserable.

When we have more, more time would be demanded of us. But, if we have less, we will have more time to do the things we truly want — and even the time to relax. After all, taking a break is also important, for even God rested on the seventh day.

Having less does not mean not buying a phone or a computer. It is not about being poor. In fact, you can be wealthy and at the same time live a simple life. It does not mean that you cannot buy the car you have always wanted or the clothes you have always wanted. Having less still means that you have and possess things — things of value and meaning, as well as things that you need to live a comfortable and good life.

When we live a simple lifestyle, we become more conscious of what we buy and the things that we keep, for we know that they can affect our life. Hence, we learn to be more responsible over the things that we choose to possess. This also allows us to live with more intent and to be conscious of what we do.

To have less means more time and more life. Having less also means having less problems to deal with and more time to do the things we love and be with the people who matter to us. Less is more because when we have less, we get more of life. We start to use the things we have and not let our things own and control us. Stop for a moment and think about this.

Live Meaningfully

Simple living encourages a life of meaning. As human beings, we have the choice to live a meaningful life. Living a meaningful life does not necessarily mean doing something out of the ordinary or spending any money. Rather, it is more about being truly present and conscious, living with intent, and a state of mind that is aware of the beauty and miracles of life. This way, every moment becomes precious — because they are, indeed, precious.

Today, many people do not honestly feel the meaning in their lives. Many end up like robots who merely exist but do not actually live. Simple living encourages us to live meaningfully and appreciate the beauty and wonder of being alive. When we live simply, we become more conscious of what happens around us. As the saying goes, we should stop and smell the roses. The simplistic approach of this lifestyle finally gives us the time to stop and smell the roses and appreciate the beauty of life. But, when we allow ourselves to be bombarded with so many things, especially with so many negative and stressful things, we miss the joy of truly experiencing what it is to be alive.

The problem with so many people these days is that we often do not have the time to breathe and be alive. Many of us are bombarded with so many things to do, people to please, more money to earn, and something else to accomplish, among others — and we become stuck in this cycle that never ends but always demands something from us.

To live simply requires us to identify the things that are important to us and to let go of the things that we do not need, especially the things that only give us stress or pull us down.

Stop for a moment and think about the things that you do not need and those things that are not important to you and yet are still present in your life. This might be the perfect time to finally throw it out into the garbage to make more space and time for yourself. Living simply is living light; the more things that you have the heavier life becomes. Choose wisely the things that you want to hold on to and be generous to let go of the things that bring you down and trap you. There is no better time to live meaningfully than now — yes, right now.

The Dangers of Consumerism

Consumerism teaches us that to be happy, we should buy more things. This is the trend that is considered normal today. Hence, many people now think more about money than the soul. Many think that if only they had more money, then they would be happy. Of course, this is a flawed way of thinking as many rich people are also sad. Money can only buy you the things that you think can make you happy — only for you to find out that it is what you need to be happy. But, of course, the world will not let you realize this; otherwise, businesses would fall. But, be very careful because this is also how the soul becomes corrupt and loses its meaning.

Consumerism is dangerous because it corrupts the soul. It makes a person very materialistic and teaches that to be happy, one should acquire more things. Indeed, we live in a world of excess. Lost in the seeming extravagance of things, man lives with the very same things that trap his soul and pull him down. You should be careful with your relationship with the things that you have. Be sure that you own and use them and not the other way around.

It should be noted that a simple life does not mean that you should not buy anything. Indeed, you will still buy things — except that you will be doing it more carefully, consciously, and with a sense of meaning and appreciation for the things that you have. You will not be buying on impulse or simply because of a mere advertisement or just to impress other people. Instead, you will buy something because it will make your life more meaningful.

Since consumerism is all about buying and acquiring new things, it forces people to get busy with how they can earn more and more money. I am not saying that money is evil, but how this kind of approach triggers people's attitude toward money is where things can become complicated, even evil. No wonder that today, many people are more interested in earning money than sincerely helping people.

When you choose the simple living approach, you should learn to see things as they are —- things. They are not life, and they are not human beings. And, things are meant to make life more beautiful and meaningful, and not lower our estimate of the importance and sacredness of human life.

Today, consumerism is the normal trend. When we choose to finally live simply and minimally, we become more conscious and responsible of our actions. We learn to think for ourselves and make our own decisions, and not just follow blindly what society tells us.

If we make our happiness depend on things, then we will never be truly happy. The reason for this is simple: Happiness is not made of things. The pleasure that we get from things is merely temporary. It fades gradually but surely. A follower of the simple living lifestyle is well aware of this, and therefore they do not depend on things to be happy. Rather, things serve their rightful purpose and remain as things to be used by a person.

It should be clarified that those who live a simple lifestyle also buy things, but they do not allow things to use them. We also should not allow our happiness to depend on things for they can easily be broken and stolen. Indeed, we can find a sense of pleasure from having something, but we should be aware that such is a mere illusion of happiness. Instead of investing in things to make us happy, we should focus on what truly lasts and what is real: we invest in good people and in building good relationships.

As you can see, if we follow the consumerism approach, it would be impossible to be truly happy. Instead, we will always be chasing the illusion of happiness. We seem to get close to it, but each time we get closer, it tends to move farther away from us.

Consumerism also makes us become obsessed with money as if earning more and more money will give us the happiness that we desire. Now, earning money is not that simple. It requires much of our time and effort. Money is also very quick to consume but takes so many hours to earn. Sadly, many people these days spend more time trying to earn money, enslaving themselves for money, only to chase a false illusion of happiness.

This does not mean that you should not engage in any kind of work. Living a simple lifestyle does not mean being lazy, but we must know the consequences and meaning of our actions; otherwise, we can easily be manipulated and be controlled by society. In the end, we might just realize that it is the world that has lived our life and that we have not made our own choices.

Consumerism also tends to make us value things over people. If this becomes our way of thinking and being, then there is no way we can be happy as we are taking a very wrong and shallow approach to life. Things should be used by people and not the other way around.

Buying things is not completely wrong. But, we should not allow ourselves to be manipulated by the system. We must not forget what is important in our life, and we ought to live a life of our own choosing.

The Beauty of Empty Space

If you take a look at minimalism art and design, you will notice something: empty space. In fact, it is the emptiness that makes it beautiful. When we live a simple lifestyle, we should also prioritize having empty spaces. This means that we should declutter our life from all the garbage, stress, as well as negative and meaningless things.

Once we create this space, it will allow us to breathe and enjoy life. But, if we bombard ourselves with so many things to do, if we allow ourselves to be manipulated by the world, then we will feel suffocated and unhappy.

But how do we create this emptiness? How can we have space in our busy life?

First, we need to recognize that we need space. Second, we should take a conscious action to create that space. Stop for a moment and think about your life. Identify the things that you have in your life that you can actually live without. Take note that these things do not only refer to objects, but also include people, situations, work, events, and negative thoughts, among others.

Second, we should make the conscious decision to drop all the things that we do not need, especially those that make us unhappy and pull us down.

Third, we should actually live our life without those things that we have decided to let go. Now, this is easier said than done.

You may find yourself still clinging to those things. Just keep on practicing, and you will soon be able to move on with your life and notice that you have more space than you used to.

This empty space should not be put to waste. This means that you should make good use of it. So what do you do with this empty space?

There are two things that you can do: first, you can leave it empty. It is strongly suggested that you make sure to have enough space in your life. It is this space that will let you breathe, as well as give you enough time to do whatever you really want to do in life. Hence, it is important to always have enough empty space in your life. Second, if you have more than enough empty space, then you can fill a part of that empty space with something nice and special.

A good exercise for this is to imagine an empty room. There is nothing in the room but emptiness. Now, one by one, start to fill this room with the things that you have and do. What are you going to place on the right side and on the left? What part of your life will be your centerpiece? Be very careful with this. Before you welcome anything in the room, examine it first if it is worth your time and if you really want to keep it. If you decide that it is necessary, helpful, meaningful, or something that you cannot live without, only then should you welcome it into your room. Take note that this will be the design and room of your life, so make sure that whatever you welcome into your room really matters to you.

When designing a room, many people wonder about the many things that they put in the room. However, it must be emphasized that preserving empty spaces is also important. If you fill the room with so many things, even if these things are very expensive, you will soon feel the room to be in so much clutter. It will be hard to move, and you may even find it difficult to breathe. It is as if every object is connected and tied to you. The more objects there are, the heavier you will feel.

This is where simply living comes in as a solution. When we take the simple lifestyle, we declutter our private and sacred space, especially from the things that are meaningless and those that only give us anxiety and stress. As we continue to live the simple lifestyle, we become lighter and lighter. We become free.

Let Go

When we shift from the influence of consumerism to the simple living approach, we need to learn how to let go. This act of letting go is good for you. It may not be easy, but it is important for your happiness.

Do not worry, you do not need to let go of the things that you love and those that are important to you. In fact, this act of letting go will allow you to give more focus and spend more time with the things that you love.

Letting go is an act of healing. By letting go of the things that trap and suffocate your soul, you can be free.

So what are these things that you need to let go of? For a start, let go of the things that only bring you negativity. Take note that things also refer to people, places, situations, and even the negative thoughts that you keep in your mind. By letting go of these sad and dark things, you can create a space in your life where life can finally enter.

The next set of things you should let go of are those that do not really cause you any harm but are simply not necessary and are only weighing you down.

I have a friend who dreams of becoming a writer. However, he has not yet written even a single book. When I asked him how he spends his time, we learned that he dedicated more time playing computer games than actually writing a book. We also learned that had he only spent even half of the time that he has already spent playing his computer game, he would have already finished writing his book.

I am not saying that we should not play computer games or that we should not entertain ourselves in any way, but we must not lose sight of our goals and dreams in life.

Needless to say, the story about my friend is only an example. If there are things that prevent you from living the life of your dream, then you should take action and exercise discipline.

Letting go is the healing act of freeing ourselves from the things that control us and hold us down. It is for our own good. By letting go, we can be free.

Free the Mind

Reality is a reflection of our mind. When we follow the simple living approach, we should also have a state of mind that would fit this kind of lifestyle. The good news is that it is actually the best state of mind to be, since simple living promotes calmness, relaxation, peace, love, and even spirituality.

When you let go of the things that you do not need, be sure not to hold on to them with your hand. A common mistake is to let go but still think about the things and people that we have chosen to let go. Once you let go, these things that you let go of do not even deserve to be remembered. Instead, you should move forward with your life with more freedom, love, and light.

Now, the mind is quite difficult to control. Even if you tell it not to think about something, the more it will remember and would even engage the subject. In fact, telling yourself not to think about something already means that you are thinking about it. So, how do you deal with the mind?

The secret lies in non-doing rather than doing. It is as simple as not thinking. Instead of getting frustrated or anything, just drop the thought in your mind right away and focus on something else. In the beginning, this may be a challenge, but you just have to give yourself enough time, and your mind will surely be able to adjust. This is a natural ability of the mind, so you do not have to worry about it.

Another thing that you can do and also something that I advise is to pray. Just give and leave all things to God. This reminds me of a verse in the Christian scripture that says, "Be still and know that I am God."

The modern world has made people believe that we should be in control, but the truth is that we are never truly in control of anything -—only God is.

When we surrender everything to God, including ourselves and all our problems and fears, then there is nothing that we should worry about. The mind becomes free, and we can focus more on enjoying the beauty of being alive.

No matter how empty you make the physical room, you will not feel any good if the mind remains cluttered with so many thoughts. Therefore, if you follow the simple living approach, you should also pay attention to the wellness of your mind.

Pay attention to the thoughts that you keep in your mind. Consider your mind as your sacred and private place. Know that nothing can exist or remain in your mind without your consent. As a basic rule, you should let go of all negative thoughts and only fill your mind with positive thoughts.

Another thing that can help with freeing the mind is the practice of meditation. Meditation connects us with our soul and frees us from destructive thoughts.

Meditation

Although not a requirement, it is still worth noting that the practice of meditation can be truly helpful with regard to freeing the mind and achieving a deeper state of spirituality. The practice of meditation can also lead us to a state of mind where we can better realize the things that we need and want in our life, as well as those that we should let go.

There are many ways to practice meditation, but you do not need to learn all of them. After all, all meditation practices lead to one and the same path, which is the path of enlightenment and divine spirituality.

The following meditation technique is an ancient practice used by Christian monks. It uses the mantra *Maranatha*, which means *Come, Lord, come, Lord Jesus*. The word *Maranatha* is in Aramaic, which is believed to be the language that was spoken by Jesus when He walked the Earth.

Before we discuss the actual meditation technique, let us first talk about certain guidelines that you need to learn about meditation.

Meditation is about stilling the mind. It is more about non-doing than doing. When you meditate, you should be as relaxed as possible. Allow the physical body to fall asleep as the mind stays awake. The more relaxed you are, the more you will reach a deeper state of mind.

Relaxation has two aspects: physical and mental. Physical relaxation is easy. You just have to assume a comfortable posture that will allow the body to relax. Among the different meditation postures or asanas, the sitting position is most ideal. It is also worth noting that the Buddha attained enlightenment as he was sitting under a tree. But, you are free to assume other postures. If you are not comfortable with the sitting position, then you can meditate while lying down, even while standing or moving. In fact, meditation can be done regardless of your body position. However, it is much easier to meditate when the body is still and relaxed.

The other aspect of relaxation is mental relaxation. Relaxing the body is easy, but relaxing the mind is often challenging. As you meditate, you may notice that thoughts keep arising in the mind, uncontrollably. You should know that this is normal, especially for beginners. The solution to this challenge is simply to keep on practicing meditation. The more that you meditate the more that the noise within the mind can be tamed. Soon enough, you will just notice that the mind is now able to become still and quiet, and this will lead you to a deep state of mind where peace and serenity are abundant.

The meditation that you are about to learn uses a mantra. A mantra is the point of focus in meditation. Instead of the mind being scattered and cluttered with so many thoughts, a mantra can be used to still the mind and only make it focus on a single point (the mantra).

The mantra that we are going to use is *Maranatha*. You should chant the mantra slowly and calmly. To help you better understand this powerful meditation, let us now head to the actual practice:

Assume a comfortable position and relax. Close your eyes and clear your mind. Start to say your mantra: Maranatha. Say it gently and lovingly. Do not imagine anything. Do not think about anything. Nothing in the mind must exist but the mantra.

If thoughts arise in the mind, ignore them. Focus only on your mantra. Your mantra is also a prayer, which makes it even more powerful. Be one with your mantra and let go of everything.

Soon enough, you will reach a deeper state of mind. The more that you practice this meditation, the more that you will reach a deeper state of mind and consciousness. It is recommended that you meditate at least twice daily.

You can end this meditation at any time by gently shifting your focus back to your physical body. To do this, you can slowly say the Our Father prayer or any other prayer that you like. You can then slowly move your fingers and toes, and then very gently open your eyes with a smile.

With regard to the length of time that you should meditate, there are no rules on it. The reason for this is that once you reach a deep state of mind, time ceases to exist. This explains how some meditators are able to meditate for very long hours.

Still, the length of time that one meditates is not a sufficient basis of one's spiritual development. Instead of focusing on the time, one should give more importance to the quality of the meditation experience.

Dealing with the Garbage

When we live a simple lifestyle, we let go of many things and hold on only to the things that are important and meaningful to us. This allows us to spend more time with those that truly deserve our attention.

In life, you will experience both good and bad, and it is up to you how you manage them. Simple living teaches us to be responsible and treat things the way they deserve to be treated.

In life, no matter how careful you are, you will still have to deal with difficult people and situations. You should be ready to face negative things every now and then. The key is to be able to manage these things properly when they come. Positive things are good, but negative things should be dealt with shrewdly.

Something that is quite irritating about negative things (and negative people) is that they are often like parasites. If you do not do anything about them, they will usually stick with you. Depending on the circumstances, you will have to deal with them from time to time. The key is to allow them to penetrate into the peacefulness of your mind. Remember that nothing can enter the sacred sanctuary of your mind without your consent. You are the master of your mind; you just have to exercise your power over it.

Let go of garbage as soon as you can. Of course, it is understandable that there will be times when you will have to deal with some garbage for some time. But, do your best not to get too attached. Focus only on what is needed and important.

Whatever it is that you have to do, just do it. It is also advisable to spend as little time as possible dealing with all the garbage, and then go back immediately into the empty space so you can breathe and relax.

Simple living also means being clear. You should be clear with your intentions and what you do. For this to be possible, you cannot be dealing with life's garbage at the same time. We have realized that there are simply things that we must let go as they are not even worth our time.

But how about the time when you need to entertain some garbage in life, such as if you happen to have a difficult boss at work or if you ever find yourself in a difficult situation that you cannot avoid?

The key is to deal with the situation and at the same time not allow yourself to be absorbed into the situation. Know that you are not a part of it. You are completely independent and on your own. Hence, no matter what other people say or even do to you or whatever happens all around you, it is up to you if you will want to make it a part of who you are. You are your own world. We do not try to control things that are outside of our realm of control; but with respect to things that are within our reach, we keep them simple, clean, and minimal. This, of course, will allow us to have more time for ourselves, think for ourselves, enjoy life, spend more time with our loved ones, and breathe freely — despite the many things that may happen all around us.

Stop

Being only human, there are times when the garbage in our lives may overtake us. When we live simply, we must learn to stop. The modern world encourages us to keep moving forward and to always be taking actions. The problem with this approach of always on the move and taking actions is that we tend to lose sight of who we really are. A simple lifestyle is simple as it is about living who you really are and not being someone whom you are not.

Sadly, many people these days are being manipulated by the modern world, and they do not even realize it. Many try so hard to impress others even though they themselves are not impressed by the very people that they are trying so hard to please.

There is a saying that we should stop and smell the roses. When we are always on the move and busy, we forget and overlook the beauty of life. Life becomes a mere boring routine where we exist but barely live. Simple living reminds us of what truly matters in life, and that we should make each moment special.

Another thing that we should stop doing is worrying. Because of so much that is going on these days, many people end up worrying ceaselessly. Worse, we often find ourselves worrying about the things that we cannot control. A simple living lifestyle is a worry-free life. We should train ourselves not to worry. And, if we ever find ourselves worrying, we ought to stop immediately and do something productive and positive instead.

There is a saying in Buddhism: "If you can solve your problem, what is the use of worrying? If you cannot solve your problem, what is the use of worrying?" This saying teaches a simple and logical lesson: No matter what, do not worry.

Worrying only bombards our minds with negative things, and oftentimes these things are outside of our control. Instead of worrying, we should take positive actions.

At any time that we find ourselves going out of balance, we must stop. By stopping and looking within ourselves, we can realize what is really happening, as well as how we must respond to the situation.

We should also stop from all things that are negative in nature. Stop being angry and disappointed, stop allowing other people to control you, stop looking down on yourself, and stop thinking too much, among other unhealthy things that we do.

When we stop from all those destructive habits, we will have the energy that we can direct for things that are positive, constructive, creative.

Of course, this is easier said than done, but it is very much within your power. Just be kind enough to yourself and give yourself time to adjust to the new habit of simple living.

On Acquiring Things

It should be clarified that simple living is not the absence of things. You will still possess things. However, instead of allowing things to own and control you, you will be more responsible and use the things that you have. Moreover, instead of being bombarded with so many things, you will keep only good and meaningful things. This way, when you look around you, there will be enough space to breathe, and at the same time, you will be surrounded only with beautiful things.

Although simple living encourages that we do not follow the consumerism approach of always resorting to buying expensive things, you are not forbidden to buy something expensive if you truly want it, and most especially if you really need it. Simple living is not about being poor. You can be rich and at the same time live a very simple lifestyle, which means a beautiful and meaningful life.

Although simple living strongly encourages having and creating space, it does not promote a total empty space. So, feel free to buy the smartphone that you want or the sofa that you love.

Although simple living also supports frugality, it is not all about being frugal. You are still free to spend money on expensive things. Now, please be mindful about this. If you can afford to be frugal, then by all means do so. It is still a really good way to apply the simple living lifestyle. But, simple living does not demand of us a hardcore approach, so do not be too hard on yourself.

It should be noted that simple living strongly encourages frugality, and must also be noted that being frugal does not mean being cheap. You are not cheap. Being frugal is about making wise decisions with respect to money and spendings. Hence, it is a good way to support the simple living lifestyle, and vice versa.

Things are supposed to help people. Although this help may not always be in a practical sense, all the things that you possess should at least be of value to you. If not, then maybe those things, whatever they may be, should be thrown away in order to create more space in your life. Again, creating and keeping space are very important in a simple living approach.

Managing a Busy Schedule

Having a schedule is not always necessary. However, if you are a busy person like myself, then having a schedule would be really helpful in order to live and maintain a simple lifestyle despite work demands and other things that require your time and attention.

These days, being busy is a common thing. It is as if it is important for you to become busy. Sadly, this is a wrong way of thinking, and no wonder that so many people in the world today are very stressed out and unhappy.

Of course, the best advice is to not allow yourself to be busy. But, if this is not possible, such as if you have a demanding work that you cannot abandon, then having a schedule would be advantageous.

Now, the important thing about setting your schedule is that you must give yourself more than enough time to comply and finish the things that you have to do. Yes, you need *more than enough time* — take note of that. This way, you will not be pressured with regard to meeting your deadlines. For example, if a certain task will require you to spend a day to finish it, give yourself two days or even three days for that task alone. Apply the same principle with the other must-do things in your schedule.

A common pitfall is procrastination. Be very cautious that you do not fall into this trap. Just because you have given yourself more time than necessary to finish doing something does not mean that you can allow yourself to be lazy and take time for granted. You should still complete the work as efficiently and early as you can. Even though you have scheduled something to be completed in three days, if you can finish it in one day, then do so. By using this approach, you can create more space in your schedule. It will also prevent you from working under pressure.

You should also avoid filling your hands with more things than you can effectively handle without sacrificing much of your time and peace of mind. Sometimes we become too greedy to earn more money that we sacrifice our peace of mind just to earn additional income. Do not forget that taking a rest is also important.

Of course, there will still be times when you have to deal with a very busy schedule. Things like this do happen, but you just avoid them from happening as much as you can. Now, in case they do happen, then remember that your mind is your private place. You can still be in a very busy place but remain peaceful and at ease in your mind. Simple living is also realizing that you ought to let go of the things outside of you and that you can cherish the peacefulness that you keep within you.

Simple and Minimal

Simple is beautiful, and minimal creates space. There are no hard and fast rules on how simple one should be. It is something that we just know for it is ingrained in our being. Even our ancestors naturally lived a simple lifestyle.

Overthinking is another pitfall that should be avoided. The modern world promotes too much heavy thinking, failing to realize that the power of the brain is very much limited. Hence, simple living encourages the use of imagination and intuition. It is as if we go back to the old days where we listen once again to what our heart tells us.

Going minimal does not mean choosing small things or going small. Rather, it is more about creating more space for art and for life. Simple and minimal come together. In fact, they are often used interchangeably. This is because they come from the same spirit, which is the art of simple living.

Here is an example of going simple and minimal: Instead of having 10 mugs to drink your morning tea or coffee, simply use one mug — the mug that you love as it was given to you by your mother or a special someone. This will not only create more physical space, but it will also bless every morning with love and good memories.

Simple living is focused on living profoundly and meaningfully. Again, it is not about being poor, but a way to live life with more intent and meaning.

Today, we are living in a world of excess. The world has taught us that in order to be happy, we should continuously consume things. It may seem that this is the right way to happiness, but the truth is that it is only an illusion of happiness. Instead of bombarding ourselves with more things to do and worry about, we should make more space and time for ourselves.

The world will do its best to keep us busy, so that we will not be able to think, and so that we will not realize just how badly and meaningless we are living our lives.

When we live life simply and minimally, we get to have more time and opportunities to live life and really think and ponder about what is happening in our lives. This gives us a chance to reflect and understand ourselves better. As you can see, living a simple life allows us to live our lives with more meaning and intention. It will save us from the evils of the manipulative modern world.

Of course, this is not something that happens on its own. We need to make the conscious decision and effort to apply it in our life. The good news is that living simply and minimally does not require so much from us. And, unlike the modern world that has ceaseless demands for our time and effort, simple living tells us to do less, spend less, and to relax more instead of being too active and busy with work.

Simple living is a fine and delicate taste that is, perhaps, not for everyone -—although it would suit all of those who seek to live a more meaningful and peaceful life. In the end, it is still up to you how you intend to make use of this way of living. The path is open, but it is your turn to take the steps and trudge on into this wonderful journey.

On Money

What is your view of money? How important is it to you? Do you consider it as a very important thing in your life? Stop for a moment and ponder about these questions. It is important that you answer these questions honestly. It is okay if you feel that you are very attracted and attached to money. After all, that is normal these days. The important thing is that you recognize such attachment, and that you are now willing to make positive changes.

A person who lives a simple lifestyle still knows that money is important. However, we also know that money is not everything. Indeed, it can give you comfort, it can give you nice and fine things, but it cannot give you true happiness. This is because true happiness is only real when you are able to share it with someone, and preferably with someone you love. Again, we are not saying that money is not important, but realize that money is not everything.

One's honest view of money can have a big impact on their personality. Those who have a close relationship with money are usually the materialistic kind of people, while those who treat money as they are — a mere object or thing — usually display a deeper sense and view of life and even spirituality.

When you follow the simple living approach, you are encouraged to treat money as it is — a mere object. Do not depend your life and happiness on it. And never forget that the moment that you become a slave to money, it would be impossible for your soul to be truly happy.

Needless to say, even those who follow a simple and minimalist living still need and use money. Money itself is not evil, but our view and attitude toward it make it so. For example, a knife is used to cook and prepare delicious meals; however, in the hands of a murderer, that same knife becomes an evil weapon.

When we live simply, we use money with more sense of responsibility. We also recognize that our relationship with money has certain limitations.

Regardless of how much money you have, you can apply simple living to how you manage your finances. As a rule, you should avoid overspending, and you should only buy the things that are important and meaningful to you. Do not forget that every object or thing that you have will demand time and attention from you. The less things you possess, the more time that you have. This also often equates to having less stress and more peace of mind, as well as time to relax.

Having a clear view of your relationship with money is crucial. Sadly, today, so many people seem to treat money as more important than helping people, and also more important than developing a good and kind character. When we follow the simple living lifestyle, we know that that is not the right approach. The more that we meditate, the more that we realize this wisdom. This is why, although not necessary, the practice of regular meditation is strongly recommended.

On Things

Simple living is not the absence of things but being more responsible over the things that you own and keep. We do not allow ourselves to be tied to the things we own. We should use our things and not the other way around.

Stop for a moment and think about the things that you own. Are all those things important to you? Do you really use them or do many of them only take so much space in your home and remain almost neglected? Our relationship with money is one thing; our relationship with things is another.

Just as we should not allow money to control us, we should also not allow things to manipulate us. Indeed, life is so much more than the things in the world. When we follow the simple living approach, we start to discover that it is more important to focus on people than things. This approach inspires and encourages us to help people. For, indeed, the true meaning of simple living goes beyond material concerns.

By focusing less on things, we can have the space and time we need to focus on ourselves, as well as the people around us. It is sad to say that many people today are more focused on things (as well as how to acquire more things) than their family and loved ones. Of course, we want to be able to provide the needs and wants of our family, but we must also be careful not to allow such desires to gain material things to dictate our way of living.

Take some time to observe the things that you own and the things that you want to buy. Take a closer look as to the importance of all these things in your life. How many of them are truly important and how many are those that you can live without? Remember that the less things you have the more time and space you can have in your life.

Today, people often buy things without thinking about buying so much. Many follow the consumerism approach where to be happy, you need to spend money and buy something. It should be noted that earning money may not also be that easy, so you should also consider the effort that you need to give in exchange for the thing that you want to buy. Is it really worth it? Of course, if you feel in your heart that it is very much worth it and that you need it, then by all means buy it — even buy it immediately. Simple living. Is not the absence of things, but just be sure that you do not end up wasting the money.

Simple living teaches us to be grateful for the things that we have. When we buy something, we feel it as a gift. It is not uncommon for people who shift to a simple living lifestyle to buy things for themselves sparingly. Hence, each time we buy something for ourselves, it becomes a meaningful act. This is in stark contrast to someone who buys too often where they almost do not feel grateful for the things that they get as it has become a normal habit.

Even if you are rich, that does not mean that you should go about squandering your money. Of course, it is your choice to do so and no one is preventing you, but also realize that your acts also reflect so much about your character.

On Spirituality

Simple living promotes spirituality. Sadly, most people are too busy these days. Thankfully, when you take the simple living approach, you will be encouraged to focus on your spirituality. This is not really a rule, but most people who take up this lifestyle end up being finally very interested in spirituality. Although the reasons for this may be unknown as the reasons may vary from person to person, it is believed that most of the time, the reason is that when you live simply, you finally create the time to really think and reflect on the meaning of life.

When people are too busy, we tend to think so little about life, even about our loved ones. But, once we gain the time to do so, and as long as we do not waste it, then our focus tends to shift into the spiritual.

But what is so good about spirituality? Here is a secret: spirituality is life. It is not just about worshiping a high Being people usually call as God, but it is more about realizing that you are a soul and that you are one with the universe.

Regardless of your religious upbringing or spiritual faith, just know that when you live simply and minimally, you can finally have the time to deal with the matters of the soul — and this might just be one of the best things you can do in life.

The Home

Those who live simply and minimally prioritize having empty spaces in their home. In a way, the way their house is arranged reflects their way of life and state of mind. The more that we go deep into this way of life, the more that we appreciate the beauty of an empty space.

An empty space is not completely nothing, but it signifies infinite possibilities. This applies to the home, as well as in life.

Simple living also teaches us that we do not really need so much to be alive and happy. Instead of adding more things that can never fully satisfy our desire for happiness, we should add more love in our relationships, and more patience and kindness.

This lifestyle helps us realize that buying things is not the way to happiness. In fact, buying more and more things will only make us busier, and these things will occupy so much of our time. Hence, the home of a minimalist is not composed of so many things, but instead you can expect for it to be simple, minimal, and very meaningful.

Today, minimalist designs are also being appreciated by many people. In a way, they are able to connect to the meaning being conveyed by the design. This is because a part of their soul understands that they also need that space and time — a time for one'a self and a time to really enjoy life with their loved ones. And, this does not even cost any money — but only time — and you can have so much of this time if you follow the simple living lifestyle.

Enjoy the Little Things

From now on, enjoy the little things — not because you are poor, but because this time you realize and know that the little things are actually special — and once you are aware of this, they also become meaningful.

Many times, we take things for granted, and we only realize how important they are when we start to lose them. Let us not wait for that moment. Simple living is so simple that we live truly as who we really are. It is time to throw away the masks that we have been wearing, and it is time to show the world who we truly are.

Greet the Sun and the birds, enjoy the stars at night, and be conscious of the air that you breathe — and be thankful that you are alive and are able to experience these things. Remember: The little things are usually the most important things. Be happy that you are with your loved ones, rejoice that you are healthy, and be glad for you are alive and you can make a difference.

The little things are usually the important things that we just keep on ignoring. When we follow the simple living approach, we recognize the importance of the little things and begin to cherish them.

Simple living teaches us to be truly human. It encourages us to love and be kind, to be good and true. It frees us from the illusions and manipulations of the world and reminds us of what really matters in life. And, another thing I like about simple living is that it is a lifestyle that is available to everyone, and you do not even need to spend money to experience it.

Are you ready to live a simple and meaningful life? If yes, then know that you have the power in your hands. Welcome — now is the time to be truly human, now is the time to be who you really are.

Did you love *Simple Living Manual*? Then you should read *Spirituality Over Suicidal Depression*[1] by C.Z. Lazarus!

[2]

I would never kill myself. Perhaps you have said this before. You might have even laughed at the idea of suicide or even considered it a mere exaggeration. You would never kill yourself — of course, you would not — until one day, you just realize that it is the most natural thing to do.

When this finally happens— tell me, now, what would you do?

Spirituality Over Suicidal Depression is a handbook on overcoming suicidal depression through spirituality. It does not matter what your religion is, for religion is made by man while

1. https://books2read.com/u/4DgQZd

2. https://books2read.com/u/4DgQZd

faith is a free gift from God. The truth is that you have a soul and that you are a spiritual being. Please do not misunderstand. You do not need to have faith at this very moment. You do not even need to believe in God, but I need you to be alive for you to find out what this journey is all about.

According to official statistics, every 40 seconds, somebody in this world dies by suicide. Honestly, I do not know why they do not make this a daily headline in the news. It is as if they do not want you to know about it, as if it was a secret that you are not supposed to know. And what is this secret? Answer: That people have been giving up and ending their lives by their own hand. Yes, this is happening, and it is continuously happening — even right now, at this very moment.

At this very moment, someone is secretly saying goodbye to their loved ones. At this very moment, someone is losing all hope, even the will to live — and the worse part is that nobody knows — and if somebody does, would they even believe and care? At this very moment, someone is crying and confused. At this very moment, someone has a blade on their wrist while another person has a rope around their neck. With just an inch away from the Angel of Death, would they choose to bid life a farewell and embrace the angel? What if you are this person? Would you hesitate or would you gladly surrender yourself and go to the point of no return?

Spirituality Over Suicidal Depression is a life manual that deals with hard facts of being alive. We shall talk about what many try to avoid and ignore. After all, how can we continue to ignore the things that make us suffer? Why should we not talk about the things that make us sad and weep? We do not need to act and appear strong before the eyes of the people, for the simple truth is that we are all suffering. One way or another, there is a part in us that is dying and is looking for help, perhaps even for salvation.

If you are feeling sad and empty, if you feel defeated by the world, and especially if you are having suicidal thoughts, then this book is for you... I am here for you. I will share with you things — sad and dark things, but also beautiful and genuine things — with a hope that by the time you finish reading this book, we can be friends in spirit — and that you may also make the same choice as I did: To choose to live and make your life meaningful. Let it overflow with goodness, wonders, and love.

Dear stranger... whoever you are... I love you.

Read more at https://www.charlzdelacruz.com/.

Also by C.Z. Lazarus

Spirituality Over Suicidal Depression
The Interactive Book of Magic for Beginners
Energy Ball Bible
Control the Fire Element with Your Mind
You are the Magic Wand
Basic Pendulum Magic for Divination
Dark Energy Mastery Manual
Christos Magick
Enochian Handbook on Dark Wizardry
The Secret Seal of Solomon, Clavicula Magus
Energy Harmony Magic
Starsoul Wizardry Handbook
Reconstructing the Mind for True Spirituality
Arcane Magic for Beginners
The Psychic Witch Handbook
Cast a Magic Circle
A Beginner's Guide to Demonic Possession & Exorcism
Simple Living Manual

Watch for more at https://www.charlzdelacruz.com/.

9 7 9 8 2 0 1 0 1 9 6 2 4